They Won One!

amicus readers

by Rebecca Felix

Ideas for Parents and Teachers

Amicus Readers let children practice reading informational texts at the earliest reading levels. Familiar words and concepts with close photo-text matches support early readers.

Before Reading
- Discuss the cover photo with the child. What does it tell him?
- Ask the child to predict what she will learn in the book.

Read the Book
- "Walk" through the book and look at the photos. Let the child ask questions.
- Read the book to the child, or have the child read independently.

After Reading
- Use the matching quiz at the end of the book to review the text.
- Prompt the child to make connections. Ask: *Can you think of other words that sound the same but have different meanings and spellings?*

Amicus Readers are published by Amicus
P.O. Box 1329, Mankato, MN 56002
www.amicuspublishing.us

Library of Congress Cataloging-in-Publication Data

Felix, Rebecca, 1984-
  They won one! / Rebecca Felix.
     pages cm. -- (Hear homophones here)
  Audience: K to Grade 3.
  Audience: Age 6
  ISBN 978-1-60753-573-7 (hardcover) --
  ISBN 978-1-60753-657-4 (pdf ebook)
  1. English language--Homonyms--Juvenile literature.
  2. Sports--Juvenile literature. I. Title.
  PE1595.F53 2014
  428.1--dc23
                                  2013048621

Photo Credits: Fuse/Thinkstock, cover, 1, 16 (bottom right), 16 (bottom left); Stockbyte/Thinkstock, 3; Steve Broer/Shutterstock Images, 4–5; Aspen Photo/Shutterstock Images, 6; Patryk Kosmider/Shutterstock Images, 8–9, 16 (top left); Vanessa Nel/Shutterstock Images, 10 (left); Steve Cukrov/Shutterstock Images, 10–11; Tungphoto/Dreamstime, 12; Catherine Yeulet/Thinkstock, 15, 16 (top right); Shutterstock Images, 16 (middle left); Steve Cukrov/Shutterstock Images, 16 (middle right)

Produced for Amicus by The Peterson Publishing Company and Red Line Editorial.

Editor Jenna Gleisner
Designer Jake Nordby
Printed in the United States of America
Mankato, MN
2-2014
PA10001
10 9 8 7 6 5 4 3 2 1

Homophones are words that sound the same. But they have different meanings and spellings. What homophones can we find in sports?

team
teem

A **team** is a group of players. To **teem** is to become very full. This stadium **teems** with people. They watch the **teams** play.

4

threw
through

The pitcher **threw** a pitch. It flew **through** the air. It went so fast the batter missed it!

course
coarse

Golf is played on a **course**. The sand on this golf **course** is **coarse**. **Coarse** means not smooth.

9

for
fore

A golfer chooses the right club **for** each shot. Watch out for the ball if a golfer yells, "**Fore!**"

ball
bawl

To **bawl** is to cry. Poor sports might **bawl** if they miss the **ball**.

one
won

Each team has **one** goalie on the field. The blue team's goalie missed the ball. The red team **won** the game!

Match each homophone to its picture!

ball

bawl

course

coarse

one

won